FORECASTING

BILL McAULIFFE

SCIENCE OF THE SKIES

Published by Creative Education
P.O. Box 227, Mankato, Minnesota 56002
Creative Education is an imprint of The Creative Company
www.thecreativecompany.us

Design and production by Liddy Walseth
Art direction by Rita Marshall
Printed by Corporate Graphics in the United States of America

Photographs by AP Images (Olivier Maire/Keystone), Alamy (Marvin Dembinsky Photo
Associates), Corbis (Ed Darack/Science Faction, Brooks Kraft, Christopher J. Morris,
NASA, Jim Reed/Science Faction, Seth Resnick/Science Faction, Michael Weber,
Staffan Widstrand), Dreamstime (Amberleaf, Davidmartyn, Luri, Stanislav Perov, Matt
Trommer, Pictureone.net, Wesfoto), Getty Images (Artic-Images, Justin Bane/US Navy,
Luis Castaneda Inc., Fabrice Coffrini/AFP, FPG, Jeff Hutchens, Joe Raedle, Erik Rank,
Erik Simonsen), iStockphoto (Donall O Cleirigh, Richard Goerg, David T. Gomez, Cathy
Keifer, Keith Webber Jr., Roger Whiteway, Andrejs Zemdega)

Library of Congress Cataloging-in-Publication Data
McAuliffe, Bill.
Forecasting / by Bill McAuliffe.
p. cm. — (Science of the skies)
Summary: An exploration of weather forecasting, including how this science has
developed in the past two centuries, vital forecasting equipment such as radar, and
possible future developments.
Includes bibliographical references and index.
ISBN 978-1-58341-927-4
1. Weather forecasting—Juvenile literature. I. Title.

QC995.43.M43 2010
551.63—dc2 2009023506

CPSIA: 120109 PO1095

First Edition
2 4 6 8 9 7 5 3 1

CREATIVE C EDUCATION

FORECASTING

BILL McAULIFFE

SCIENCE OF THE SKIES

THE WARNINGS WERE ALREADY BLARING ACROSS TELEVISION SCREENS, RADIO BROADCASTS, AND NEWS WEB SITES: BLIZZARD! STRANGELY, THERE WAS NOTHING ON **RADAR** BETWEEN WISCONSIN AND THE MEXICAN BORDER. "ANOTHER JOKE BY THOSE FORECASTERS?" SOME PEOPLE WONDERED. THE NEXT DAY, THE STORM HIT THE UPPER MIDWEST WITH ALL THE WIND AND SNOW THAT HAD BEEN PREDICTED. DECADES BEFORE, PEOPLE MIGHT HAVE DIED IN SUCH A STORM, CAUGHT OUTDOORS OR TRAVELING. BUT IN EARLY 2007, FORECASTERS WERE ABLE TO DESCRIBE THE FEBRUARY 28–MARCH 2 BLIZZARD MANY HOURS BEFORE IT TOOK SHAPE. PLOWING CREWS GOT ORGANIZED. PEOPLE LEFT WORK EARLY. AND TO THE DELIGHT OF THOUSANDS OF STUDENTS, SCHOOL WAS CALLED OFF. WHAT HAD BEEN ONLY A COMPUTERIZED PREDICTION 24 HOURS BEFORE BECAME A MASSIVE BLIZZARD BUT NO GREAT DISASTER. IT WASN'T MAGIC—MERELY AN EXAMPLE OF HOW WEATHER FORECASTING CONTINUES TO LET PEOPLE KNOW A LITTLE MORE ABOUT TOMORROW THAN THEY KNEW YESTERDAY.

SAILORS' DELIGHT

Humans have always wanted to foretell the future. Through the ages, people who were thought to have special powers made predictions about the rise and fall of kings and queens or about health, wealth, love, marriage, or children. But most of the time, people have just wanted to know if it was going to rain on the next day's picnic. It's that constant interest that has kept people trying to figure out what the weather will do next.

Through centuries of experimentation, observation, and experience, and with improvements in equipment, scientists have become better at forecasting the weather. And because so many things in the modern world—agriculture, transportation, recreation, construction, water management, and even school schedules—depend on accurate weather forecasts, scientists keep working to get it right.

People have long used the things they could see or feel to predict the weather. Homemade weather prediction methods have grown out of the apparent connections between weather and the responses of plants, the behavior of animals, and even the moisture on rocks. If people's joints or teeth ached, that supposedly meant a change in the weather was on its way. The clouds, the color of the sunset, or how high the birds were flying have also been used as weather indicators. If people wanted to assess long-term weather, such as whether a cold winter or a good growing season was coming, they even looked at the skin on onions. And they often made rhymes to help them remember the advice. For example:

> *Onion skins very thin,*
> *Mild winter coming in.*
> *Onion skins thick and tough,*
> *Coming winter cold and rough.*

For many centuries, when distant travel was by ship and some of the keenest weather observations were by sailors, forecasting was simply about watching the sky.

Scientists believe that many animals and birds, including peacocks (above), are sensitive to the changes in air pressure that usually accompany approaching storms.

In centuries past, sailors at sea were probably the best weather observers. They could see more of the sky for more of the time than people on land and even watched it all night as they **navigated** by the positions of the stars. It was sailors who handed down probably the best-known weather clue:

Red sky at night, sailors' delight.
Red sky at morning, sailors take warning.

This weather **proverb** has endured because it is so frequently accurate. A red sky at night is often the result of the setting sun breaking through clouds just as they are parting in the west, indicating clearer weather is on its way. A red sky at morning often occurs as the rising sun's rays light up low clouds closing in on the eastern horizon, sealing the sky and strongly suggesting a day of rain and possibly storms.

Hundreds of other weather proverbs have also been reliable indicators of weather. One goes:

When the peacock loudly bawls,
Soon we'll have both rain and squalls.

This reflects the fact that livestock and domestic animals often get restless and agitated in the hours before a storm. Plants, too, often get credit for their

UPS AND DOWNS OF FORECASTING

*Every day, at the same moment around the world, helium-filled balloons carrying weather instruments are set aloft from 800 locations, including 92 in the U.S. and its territories and 31 in Canada. The balloons start out six feet (1.8 m) wide. They can ascend to 115,000 feet (35,000 m), travel 180 miles (290 km), and encounter temperatures of −130 °F (−90 °C). In light air pressure at high **altitude**, the balloons might expand to 25 feet (7.6 m) wide before bursting. The instruments, in a package the size of a large shoebox, fall with parachutes; 20 percent are recovered and reused.*

role as weather forecasters, as in this proverb:

If the weather you would tell,

Look at the scarlet pimpernel.

The tiny red flower, common across North America, Europe, and Asia, is also known as the poor man's **barometer** or the shepherd's weather glass, because of its habit of closing its petals when rain approaches and opening them for fair weather.

The Zuni Indians, a tribe in the deserts of the American Southwest, didn't need a rhyme to be alert to rain. But they did note that when locks of hair on the enemy scalps they had collected became damp, rain was likely. Hair's response to humidity, or an abundance of water vapor in the air, has actually been put to use in meteorology. Because hair lengthens in moist air and shortens in drier air, devices since the 18th century have used hair, attached to levers and a pen, to track humidity levels on paper.

H. H. C. Dunwoody, chief of the United States Army Signal Service, the predecessor of the U.S. Weather Bureau (which was renamed the National Weather Service in 1970), noted in 1883 that even the best meteorologists of the day were "still unable to give reliable forecasts of the weather for a longer period

One of the world's most useful plants for primitive weather monitoring, the scarlet pimpernel is a shallow-rooted flower found widely across the world.

than two or three days, and frequently not longer than twenty-four hours." He called for further research into the behavior of plants and animals as a way to improve weather forecasting.

It's unlikely that modern forecasters would examine rocks or see if barnyard animals were all facing one way, as animals sometimes do before changes in the weather, prior to making a weather prediction. Forecasters instead turn to satellite readings, radar, a network of weather sensors around the world, and instant global communications. But merely by watching the atmosphere close to the ground and in the sky, anybody can make weather predictions. It helps to be able to identify some cloud types and know where north, south, east, and west are. After that, there are some basic patterns to the weather that occurs across much of North America:

• If cumulus clouds—the classic, puffy clouds of summer—travel alone across the sky on a west or northwest wind, and any morning fog burns off by noon, fair weather will continue through the day and possibly even into the next day.

• If cumulus clouds have formed towers by noon, or joined together, or if a south wind picks up speed, it's going to rain soon. Wind shifting in a counterclockwise direction indicates a low-pressure system moving through the region, bringing unsettled or stormy weather.

• If a halo around the moon, created by high-altitude ice crystals, is shrinking or close to the moon, rain or snow will arrive in about 12 hours.

Weather watchers along ocean coasts find cues in the behavior of birds; water-going birds such as pelicans often head inland when weather is about to become severe.

- South winds shifting to the west, along with a lifting cloud ceiling, mean clear skies are on the way.

- Expect a cool night if the sky is clear and winds are light.

- If clouds of different types are traveling in different directions at different levels, it's a safe bet that the weather is about to get worse and possibly severe.

- Heavy banks of dark clouds on the western horizon mean rain or thunderstorms are coming.

That's a lot to keep track of. Many people jot their weather observations in notebooks and journals, which, over time, helps reveal patterns. Years of observation also help. Meanwhile, science continues to examine causes and effects of changes in the atmosphere. The weather is there for all to see, but even after centuries of trying to predict what's to come, few people are truly good at it.

Because clouds act as a kind of insulator, trapping warmth next to the earth, a clear night sky void of cloud cover typically means that temperatures will be cool or cold.

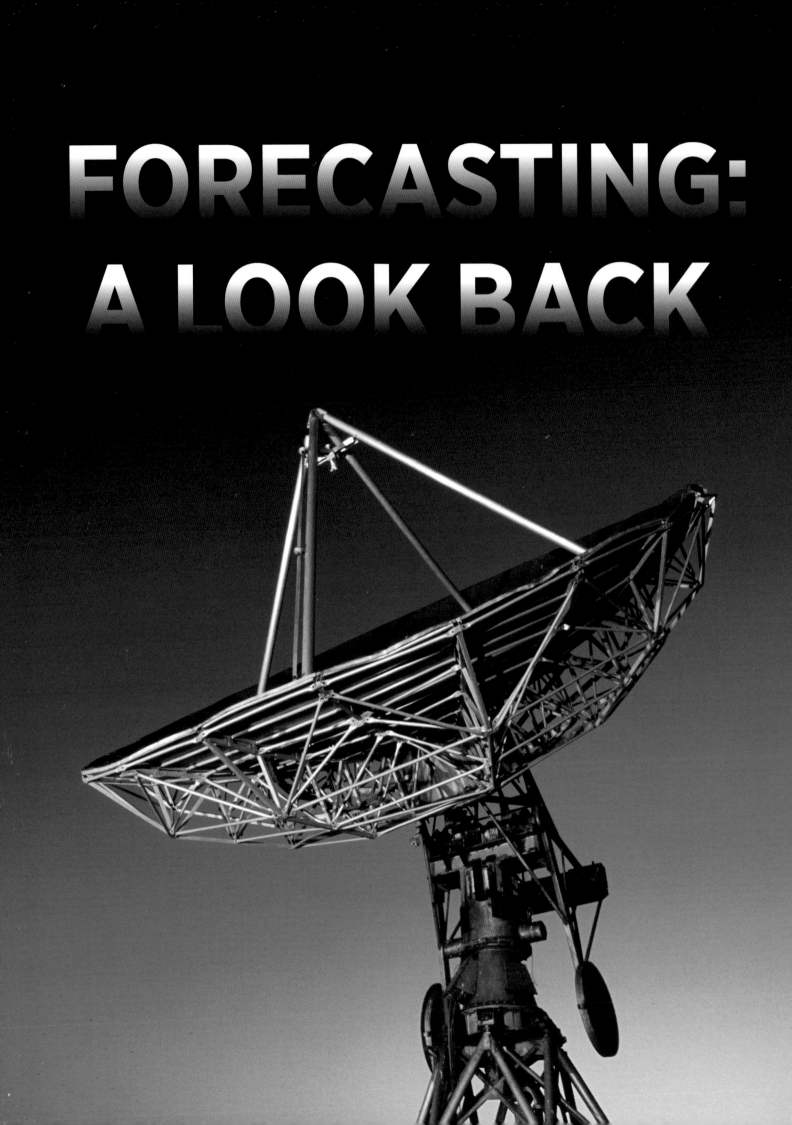

More than 2,000 years ago, the Greek scholar Aristotle began to give shape to a field of study he called "meteorology," which dealt with a wide range of dynamics of the earth and sky. He wrote about winds, thunder, lightning, rainbows, meteors, and the Milky Way, which he took to be a **phenomenon** in Earth's atmosphere rather than a galaxy in deep space. Remarkably, he also outlined how water will **evaporate** and rise, then **condense** into clouds and finally fall back to Earth again—a cycle that is one of the most basic factors in the weather we experience.

Today, relying on a dense distribution of weather observers around the world and using radar to sweep the skies and detect precipitation and severe weather, meteorologists can still get a forecast wrong, and they are regularly ridiculed for it. "I've always said that to be a weather forecaster, you need a science degree, but you really need a thick skin," said David Phillips, senior climatologist for Environment Canada, which runs the nation's forecasting service. For early meteorologists especially, weather had much less science behind it than it does today—and even less certainty.

The barometer was invented in 1643, but scientists still didn't have many clues about how storms formed or how they moved across continents. A century later, American statesman and inventor Benjamin Franklin

compared accounts of stormy weather in Philadelphia, Pennsylvania, and Boston, Massachusetts, and established the breakthrough notion that storms travel with their own winds.

Two millennia before the invention of radar antennas helped clarify weather processes, Aristotle (above) laid a foundation for our understanding of the skies and space.

THE CRICKETOMETER

*Meteorologists depend on balloons, thermometers, barometers, **anemometers**, and other "-ometers" to tell them what the current weather conditions are. But they can also use crickets. Crickets chirp at different rates corresponding to the temperature—faster when it's warm, slower when it's cool. In fact, the number of cricket chirps in 15 seconds, plus 40, equals the temperature in Fahrenheit. So if a cricket chirps 25 times in 15 seconds, it's 65 °F. Fifteen chirps means it's 55 °F. It's easier, of course, to use the National Weather Service's online "Cricket Chirp Converter." The hard part might be pinpointing the sound of just one single cricket.*

In Canada, a government meteorological observatory was established in Toronto, Ontario, in 1839. American meteorologists began developing nationwide weather tracking and forecasting systems soon after. In the 1850s, Joseph Henry, a **physicist** who had helped Samuel Morse develop the telegraph and who was also director of the Smithsonian Institution in Washington, D.C., persuaded the institution to supply weather instruments to telegraph operators across the U.S. Nearly 600 operators wired their daily reports to the Smithsonian. From these, Henry produced national weather maps and displayed them in the Smithsonian, where the daily maps were dotted with white disks to indicate fair weather, blue to denote snow, black for rain, and brown for cloudy conditions. The maps became popular with tourists, who, Henry said, "all appear to be specially interested in knowing the condition of weather to which their friends at home are subjected at the time."

Henry made his maps available to the *Washington Evening Star*, which, in May 1857, became the first newspaper in the U.S. to print a national weather map. Henry himself became so confident in his system that he would postpone giving evening lectures in Washington, D.C., if there had been rain indicated on the map in Cincinnati, Ohio, that morning.

Henry became an advocate for a government-sponsored weather and storm-prediction agency. The use of the telegraph to report and forecast weather was disrupted by the Civil War, which was fought from 1861 through 1865. But soon after the war, in 1870, president Ulysses S. Grant established the U.S. Army Signal Service. The agency, led by meteorological scholar Cleveland Abbe, developed advanced weather mapping and posted maps and warnings in public places in major cities twice a day. In 1891, weather forecasting duties in the U.S. were handed from the Signal Service to the U.S. Weather Bureau, an office of the Department of Agriculture.

Meanwhile, to the north, Canada's size and wildness limited the growth of weather communications. In the 1880s, Canadian railroads began attaching signs with one-word forecasts to trains headed east to inform the few people along the lines about what weather was coming. Daily forecasts weren't developed for parts of Saskatchewan and Alberta until 1903.

But by 1900, the advance of radio dramatically expanded the practice of weather observing, with forecasts and observations traveling to and from North America, Europe, Asia, and ships at sea. But the forecasts were still error-filled. Meteorologists in the U.S. and Europe had begun to think that the flow of

The barometer (above), which was developed in the mid-17th century, helped to confirm that clouds and air have weight, a notion that greatly furthered meteorology.

air high above the earth might have something to do with weather, and had been using kites and balloons to track conditions up to about 45,000 feet (13,700 m) by the late 1890s. But everyday forecasters knew little or nothing about the much higher-altitude air streams and other upper air movements, and they continued to depend on air pressure readings on their maps, along with wind directions. They also believed that storms generally followed established routes.

During World War I, fought from 1914 to 1918, the U.S. and England stopped distributing general Atlantic Ocean weather information because they suspected the Germans had been using it to plan bombing flights by dirigibles over England. But that left Norwegian fishermen without useful weather information. Using a network of observers along their western coast, the Norwegians, led by meteorologist Jacob Bjerknes, established the idea that precipitation occurs where warm air and cold air meet. Since it was wartime, they described this as a clash of "fronts" and developed the graphic descriptions—blue lines with forward-pointing blade-tips for cold fronts, and red lines with rounded bumpers for warm fronts—that are still used on surface weather maps today.

Soon after the war, airplanes proved invaluable in weather observing. Also, in 1927, two French scientists

BRING AN EXTRA JACKET

Every autumn, The Old Farmer's Almanac *publishes weather forecasts for 16 regions of the U.S. for the next calendar year. Its "secret formula" goes back to 1792 but still relies on solar activity combined with long-term weather tendencies. The Almanac claims an 80 percent accuracy rate for its forecasts, some for dates 15 months ahead. Most professional meteorologists say that forecasts are unreliable more than eight days in advance. The Old Farmer's Almanac predicted "Sunny, mild" for the U.S. presidential inauguration in Washington, D.C., on January 20, 2009. Under partly cloudy skies, the temperature at noon was 15 °F (8.3 °C) below normal.*

developed a device called a radiosonde, which could be carried to much higher altitudes by unmanned balloons, take weather readings, and transmit them by radio back to meteorologists on the ground. Radiosondes could also be tracked by radio, so meteorologists could determine exactly where the readings were coming from, a new breakthrough.

World War II, which featured even more planes in the air and ships at sea, brought about new advances in weather forecasting. American pilots on high-altitude bombing runs to Japan noted extremely strong headwinds, soon to be called the jet stream. Meteorologists suddenly had a much better grasp of the full dimensions of weather systems—their vast circular size, the length of cold and warm fronts extending across states and countries, and now their height. It was now clear that, because so many readings were necessary for accurate forecasts, meteorologists were going to need some new tools to manage the information. Someone needed to invent a computer.

Forecasting took a huge step forward with the advent of the airplane, which can drop loads—from bombs to weather instruments—from high in the atmosphere.

PLENTY OF HOMEWORK

To be a government meteorologist in the U.S. or Canada, a person must have a college degree in meteorology, also known as atmospheric sciences. Getting that degree requires studying basic aspects of weather as well as some combination of physics, math, radar and satellite technology, water resources, oceanography, geography, and even electricity, magnetism, statistics, and **optics**. *It's also helpful to delve into computer science. To become television meteorologists, students need to study communications in addition to meteorology. In Canada, it's also very helpful to know the French language, since just under one quarter of Canadian people speak French.*

One of Jacob Bjerknes's insights into weather prediction in the 1920s was the idea that storms traveled in much the same way water or even heat moves. This idea took forecasting in a new direction. Previously, all weather forecasting was based on observation of the actual conditions from place to place—clouds, winds, temperature, barometric pressure, rain, or snow. This was called synoptic meteorology. Bjerknes instead tried applying the laws of physics to weather prediction.

In 1922, an English mathematician named Lewis Fry Richardson proposed something similar. After successfully predicting the pattern and speed of water flowing through **peat**, Richardson came to believe that weather behaved similarly and could be predicted using mathematical **equations**. If he knew a set of atmospheric conditions, Richardson reasoned, he could calculate how they would behave as time passed and they continued to move. Richardson's forecast, being experimental, was based on readings taken across Europe at 7:00 A.M. on May 20, 1910, a day 12 years earlier. He wanted to "predict" air pressure and winds three hours later. Because he knew what actually had happened, he could check whether his forecast process worked. One reason he chose a 3-hour lead time was that he estimated that predicting weather 24 hours later would become so complicated that it would require 60,000 people doing individual math problems.

Richardson did his own calculations on paper. The effort first became famous because it was wildly wrong, predicting a dramatic rise in air pressure when no such rise had happened. Decades later, though, scientists found that if Richardson had carried the mathematical process one step farther, his **numerical forecast** would have been accurate.

Just after World War II, researchers at Princeton University realized that computers—a developing technology—would have their greatest impact if they were used in weather forecasting, because of the volume of data involved. By 1950, meteorologists had generated

Radio telescopes are among the most powerful means of long-distance observation, enabling scientists to peer into both space and the upper reaches of the atmosphere.

a successful forecast with the Electronic Numerical Integrator and Computer (ENIAC). Unfortunately, it took 24 hours to forecast weather 24 hours ahead. Two years later, they had it down to five minutes. By the end of the 1960s, computers were making better upper-air forecasts than meteorologists.

At about that same time, though, another scientist challenged the very foundations of weather's predictability. Edward Lorenz, a mathematician, had served as an Army Air Force forecaster during World War II. In 1972, he asserted that even if data from evenly spaced weather observation stations around the world were known, tiny fluctuations and changing elements of the ever-moving atmosphere between them would go unnoticed. That would build errors into computers' calculations, and those errors would multiply with each step. More than two centuries after meteorologists began to think they could predict how weather behaved, Lorenz had introduced the idea of chaos into forecasting. He summarized his ideas in a paper entitled, "Predictability: Does the Flap of a Butterfly's Wings in Brazil set off a Tornado in Texas?" His idea became known as "The Butterfly Effect," in which a

small change in conditions can lead to large-scale occurrences and huge errors in prediction.

Forecasters have continued trying to narrow the gap between calculations and chaos. In the late 1960s, a young National Weather Service forecaster named Rich Naistat, working at the agency's Techniques Development Laboratory in Silver Spring, Maryland, was pulled aside by a veteran meteorologist and told there was no future for forecasters, since computers were doing all the work. Naistat ignored the advice and went on to become science and operations officer at the Minneapolis–St. Paul office of the Weather Service, exploring new technology and forecasting techniques and teaching both young and experienced forecasters. He retired in 2007. "We were still putting forth a product and service that was better than the computer itself," Naistat said, explaining how he

Since computers were first used to help predict cloud and wind behavior, the technology has become indispensable in research stations (opposite) around the world.

RIGHT, LEFT, FORWARD!

In 1857, a Dutch meteorologist named Buys Ballot published a handy way to determine air pressure without any tools. Stand with the wind at your back. Though you can't feel it, lower pressure will be on your left and higher pressure on your right. It's the opposite in the Southern Hemisphere. This is because wind travels counterclockwise around low-pressure centers in the Northern Hemisphere (and, of course, the opposite in the Southern Hemisphere). Ballot's "law" was developed to help ships at sea navigate away from the centers of storms and from the sides where winds are strongest: right in the north, left in the south.

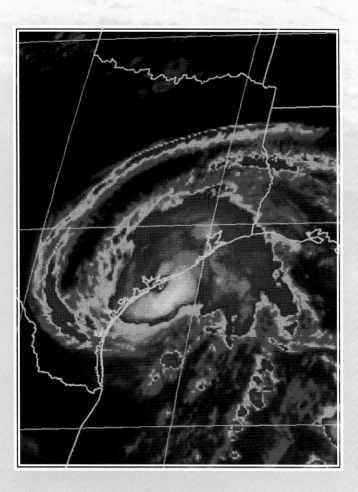

believed even 40 years ago that the human element would remain critical in forecasting.

Today's weather forecasts take into account the Butterfly Effect. Forecasters often use predictions made by computers implementing different approaches or formulas. If the computers agree, that consensus view is usually what's forecast. If they don't, forecasters might pick and choose elements of several computers' work in something called an **ensemble** forecast.

Meteorologists aren't always completely confident in their forecasts; in fact, the National Weather Service publishes the level of confidence it has in any forecast in the "Forecast Discussion" segments on its Web site. Often, if meteorologists disagree sharply with the computer runs, they return to old-fashioned methods, assessing the present conditions themselves and looking for similarities in past situations. In the end, they'll mix their own sense of the conditions with gut feelings and make a forecast. "What's really important is the experience of the forecaster who has looked back over his mistakes and was willing to learn from them," said Naistat, who, one night in January 1982, predicted 1 to 3 inches (2.5–7.5 cm) of snow for Minneapolis and St. Paul and woke up to find more than 17 inches (43.5 cm), the fourth-largest single snowfall in the metropolitan area's history.

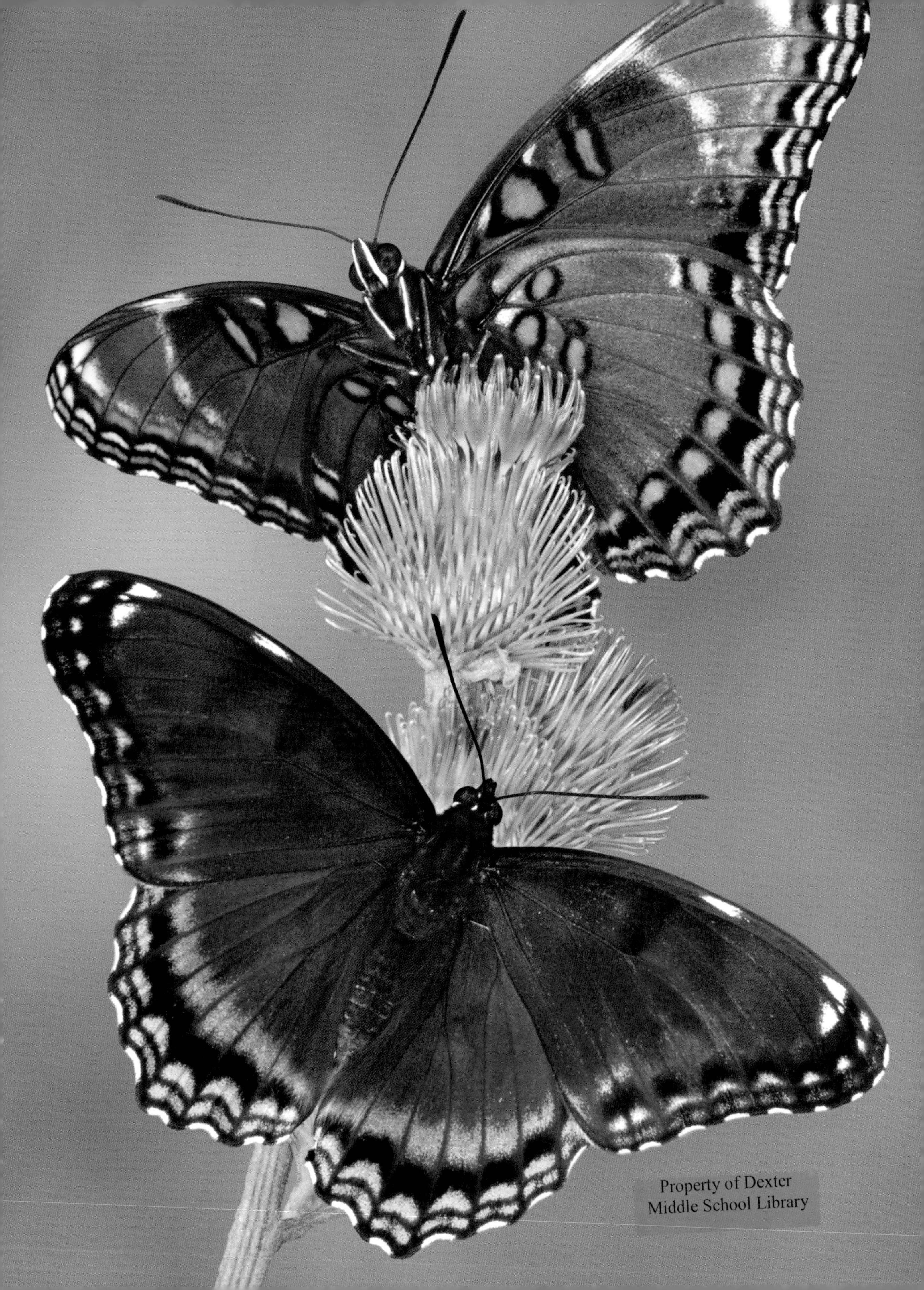

A MATTER OF INCHES

Air pressure, a key weather indicator, is often measured in "inches of mercury." This goes back to 1643, when Italian physicist and mathematician Evangelista Torricelli inserted a tube into a dish containing the liquid element mercury. Air pressure on the mercury in the dish pushed the mercury up in the tube, or let it fall, in line with changes in the atmosphere. Because the impact is greater on a small amount of mercury than on water, the mercury device could be a convenient size. A rise or fall of one inch (2.5 cm) of mercury means a significant change in the weather. Average barometric pressure at sea level is 29.92 inches (75.99 cm).

Indeed, one of the most valuable computers forecasters have today, Naistat said, is the opposite of a forecasting tool. It's something known as a weather event simulator. This device can replay radar, satellite, and other readings from past storms, allowing forecasters to see things they might have missed, study things that surprised them, and figure out how they could have made better forecasts and handled warnings.

Even with today's extensive networks of observers, sophisticated radar and computers, and forecasters who are highly educated, weather forecasting is a long way from perfect. But it's improving. In 2007, the American Meteorological Society reported that 48-hour precipitation forecasts had become as accurate as 24-hour forecasts had been a decade before. Three-day forecasts of one inch (2.5 cm) or more of precipitation were as accurate as two-day forecasts had been in 1998, and lead time on winter storm watches had increased 70 percent since 1999. Moreover, the **skill** of five-day forecasts had more than doubled since the late 1970s.

Even for tornado warnings—which are both the shortest-term weather forecasts and perhaps the most critical—lead time increased from 5 minutes to 13 minutes between 1986 and 2004. That is even after taking into account tornadoes that touched down without

warning. But for routine daily temperature and precipitation predictions, forecasts more than eight days out are still not considered reliable.

Precision instruments have long been critical to professional weather forecasting, taking readings of such conditions as humidity and wind speed and direction.

Just as the leading edges of air masses were named during wartime as "fronts," so weather forecasting has adopted another feature that first had a military use: radar. Radar, which stands for Radio Detecting and Ranging, was invented in Germany by engineer Christian Huelsmeyer in 1904. Scientists in several countries expanded on it, and the British were the first to use it for defense in wartime. During World War II, radar operators who were responsible for monitoring the movement of enemy aircraft found it difficult to spot planes amid precipitation on their radar screens, and they tried to get rid of storm images. But after the war, the storms were exactly what forecasters and others wanted to see on radar.

In 1954, a group in Illinois trying to use radar to measure rainfall rates discovered the **hook echo**, which is now used to trigger tornado warnings. Still, weather radar wasn't put to use by the government until 1957, at the National Hurricane Center in Miami, Florida. The WSR-57 (Weather Surveillance Radar, 1957) sent out short bursts of radio waves from a rotating dish antenna, and when the signals hit an object, such as a raindrop, some of the energy bounced back in proportion to the size of the object. This enabled meteorologists to track hurricanes without having to rely on reports from planes and ships.

Soon there were 66 WSR-57s at National Weather Service offices around the country, and although they remained a valuable forecasting tool for 30 years, they revealed their drawbacks as time and technology marched on. The positions of the huge antennas had to be changed with hand cranks, and the images they produced on the radar screens were blobs of green that required a highly trained eye to interpret. Someone had to watch the screen constantly and trace details on the glass with a **grease pencil**.

Beginning in 1964, scientists began to combine radar with the Doppler effect, in which the pitch of a sound changes with motion and location from the listener. Doppler radar was able to detect the motion of raindrops and hail within a storm system. Motion both

Perhaps more than any other meteorological event, tornadoes spurred the development of weather radar, as twisters can drop suddenly from supercell thunderstorms.

toward and away from the antenna indicated rotation, a key feature of major thunderstorms as well as tornadoes. Scientists tested a Doppler radar device in Norman, Oklahoma, beginning in the spring of 1971. Two years later, Doppler radar and a team of storm chasers were able to document the entire life cycle of a devastating tornado near Oklahoma City. Doppler radar's abilities were a major breakthrough in severe weather detection.

In the 1980s, forecasters acquired another tool: dual-polarization radar, which enabled them to identify different shapes of precipitation in a storm. It also distinguished between liquid and ice, telling forecasters whether the storm would drop primarily round hail or flatter raindrops.

By the mid-1990s, there were 150 Doppler units called WSR-88s (Weather Surveillance Radar, 1988) in use by the National Weather Service across the U.S. Dozens more were employed by television meteorologists, who could now broadcast full-color weather readings into people's homes.

Since 2000, storm researchers have been developing phased array radar, another spin-off from the military,

which uses multiple radar impulses. Phased array radar can perform an entire **scan** of the sky in one minute—about one-sixth the time required for other radar devices, according to the National Oceanic and Atmospheric Administration. Phased array radar can also take distant readings closer to the ground than most other radar. It is not expected to be in full use until about 2015.

In 2008, meteorologists in Oklahoma began experimenting with Collaborative Adaptive Sensing of the Atmosphere (CASA) radar. This is a system of low-cost but quick-reading radar devices that can attach to cell phone towers and fill in the gaps in the sightlines of other, larger forms of radar.

Radar is a key tool in forecasting severe weather or conditions a day or so in advance, but other technologies are needed for the longer-term view, as well as for the wider and deeper views of the atmosphere. Satellites, in orbit above Earth, provide those views. Satellites have been used to monitor weather since the 1960s. They are able to measure conditions in the atmosphere from top to bottom, as well as see hurricanes develop and track dust storms and ash plumes from volcanoes. Some also are able to forecast "space weather"—bursts of energy from the sun that can disrupt communications and electrical grids on Earth.

Besides radar, forecasters today rely on "eyes in the sky," including those of the many pilots involved in air travel, as well as the lenses of weather satellites (above).

Because they also feature communications equipment, weather satellites are often used to help with search-and-rescue operations at sea. Weather satellites are also simply great entertainment, offering up-to-the-minute views of Earth, including clouds, polar ice, and lightning. Images from hundreds of these satellites are available on the Internet.

An old forecasting technique—flying into weather disturbances—has also been revived in recent years. Researchers in 2008 began testing the use of robotic planes in forecasting. The idea is to have many small planes—ranging from about 40 pounds (18 kg) to less than 2.2 pounds (1 kg)—in the air at the same time chasing storms. Scientists believe the planes might be able to fill in the gaps in what other weather devices see in the atmosphere, thereby improving short-term forecasts.

Accurate long-term predictions remain a challenge for weather forecasters. Farmers, as well as utilities and transportation companies, would like to know more about rain, snow, heat, or cold in the months ahead. Today, forecasters such as the National Climate Prediction Center issue outlooks for weather months in advance. The outlooks describe the possible weather in terms of how likely it is that there will be more or less precipitation than normal, or how likely it is to be hotter or colder than normal.

SIDEWAYS MAPPING

Television meteorologists not only have to know what's where on a map, they have to know where things are sideways. That's because studios use a chroma-key, a special effect that allows viewers to see a vivid or moving map behind the weathercaster, where there is actually a solid blue or green wall. The trick for the meteorologist is to look at a television, usually down to the side, where he or she can see the map, and point to places on the blank wall that line up with places on the map. Rule number one: When standing next to a map of North America, the Gulf of Mexico is at the bottom.

GET YOUR OWN FORECASTER

Most people are familiar with meteorologists through the National Weather Service, television, and radio. But there are hundreds of companies that forecast weather specifically for clients in agriculture, energy, transportation, construction, and even for sports teams and events. Some companies, such as airlines, have their own forecasters to meet their own specific forecasting interests. That phone call from the dugout during a baseball game in Boston, Massachusetts, for example, might be to the team's forecaster, seeking information on approaching weather. From the late 1990s through 2007, the number of private meteorologists in the U.S. almost tripled, to more than 7,000.

To learn more, long-term forecasters have been focusing on what they call teleconnections—relationships between conditions in the atmosphere over long distances and among different features of the earth. The best-known of these are El Niño and La Niña, changes in the temperature of the Pacific Ocean along the **equator**. The two conditions, which alternate in cycles over the course of several years, can change wind and air pressure patterns and cause drought and storms all over the globe.

Meteorologists continue to pursue the elusive ability to predict the future. After centuries of study and the continuous development of new technology, forecasters are still a long way from completely understanding the complex interactions in the atmosphere. But just as our parade of weather never ends, neither will the effort to better see what's coming.

Much has been learned about the science of the skies through the use of such technologies as air-dropped research instruments (opposite), but many ways of the weather remain a mystery.

ALTITUDE, n. — *height or distance above the ground*

ANEMOMETERS, n. — *devices that measure wind speed, often with four cups rotating on a spindle*

BAROMETER, n. — *a device that measures atmospheric pressure, usually using mercury that moves up or down in a tube*

CONDENSE, v. — *to form a liquid from a vapor*

ENSEMBLE, n. — *a unit or group of parts that contribute to a single effect, as in clothes, musicians, or computerized weather forecasts*

EQUATIONS, n. — *arrangements of numbers and mathematical symbols in which one side equals the other*

EQUATOR, n. — *the imaginary line around the center of the globe, halfway between the North and South poles*

EVAPORATE, v. — *to turn from a liquid into a vapor*

GREASE PENCIL, n. — *a pencil of compressed grease and colored material used for writing on glossy surfaces*

HOOK ECHO, n. — *an electronic image, created by the bounce-back of a radar beam from a storm, that often indicates the formation of a tornado*

NAVIGATED, v. — *found a route from one place to another*

NUMERICAL FORECAST, n. — *a type of weather forecast derived from mathematical calculations rather than from observations and historical patterns*

OPTICS, n. — *the branch of physics that deals with light and vision*

PEAT, n. — *vegetable matter, usually in the form of moss, found in swampy regions called bogs*

PHENOMENON, n. — *an observable event or occurrence*

PHYSICIST, n. — *a scientist who studies physics, the science of how matter and energy interact*

PROVERB, n. — *a short saying, widely popular, that expresses a truth or fact*

RADAR, n. — *a system that uses radio waves bounced off objects, such as planes or raindrops, to determine their location, size, and speed; the word stands for Radio Detecting and Ranging*

SCAN, n. — *a full sweep of one level of the sky by a radar antenna*

SKILL, n. — *a comparison of accuracy between different forecasting techniques*

American Meteorological Society. "Weather Analysis and Forecasting." AMS Council. http://www.ametsoc.org/POLICY/2007weatheranalysisforecasting.html

Cobb, Susan. "History of Weather Radar." *NOAA Magazine*, October 29, 2004. http://www.magazine.noaa.gov/stories/mag151.htm.

Hodgson, Michael. *Basic Essentials Weather Forecasting*. 2nd ed. Guilford, Conn.: Globe Pequot Press, 1999.

Monmonier, Mark. *Air Apparent: How Meteorologists Learned to Map, Predict, and Dramatize Weather*. Chicago: University of Chicago Press, 1999.

Murphree, Tom, and Mary K. Miller. *Watching Weather*. New York: Henry Holt, 1998.

National Weather Service. "Homepage." National Oceanic and Atmospheric Administration. http://www.nws.noaa.gov.

Signal Service. *Weather Proverbs of 1883*. Washington, D.C.: Government Printing Office, 1883.

Williams, James Thaxter. *The History of Weather*. Hauppauge, N.Y.: Nova Science Publishers, 1999.

INDEX